At the Airport

Paul Humphrey

Photography by Chris Fairclough

W

FRA

First published in 2005 by
Franklin Watts
338 Euston Road
London NW1 3BH

Franklin Watts Australia
Hachette Children's Books
Level 17/207 Kent Street
Sydney NSW 2000

ISBN-13: 978 0 7496 6188 5

Dewey classification number: 387.7'89

Planning and production by Discovery Books Limited
Editor: Rachel Tisdale
Designer: Ian Winton
Photography: Chris Fairclough
Series advisors: Diana Bentley MA and Dee Reid MA
Fellows of Oxford Brookes University

The author, packager and publisher would like to thank the following
people for their participation in this book: Joanne, Steve, Josh and George
Birch; Sonia Ely and staff at Liverpool John Lennon Airport; EasyJet; Travelex;
The United Kingdom Passport Service.

Printed in China

Contents

Josh and his family are at the airport.

The check-in assistant looks at their tickets and passports.

He weighs their bags.

MAX 150.0Kg
MIN 2.0Kg
e = 0.1Kg

Weigh item 3

13.4 kg

He gives
them their
boarding
cards.

They go through security ...

... and then to passport control.

They change their
English pounds into
money to spend
in Spain.

While they wait for the plane, they go to the café.

Thank you.

Time	Flight	Destination	Gate	Remarks
13:00	EZY7103	GENEVA	20	BOARDING
13:10	EZY7181	MADRID	17	BOARDING
13:50	EZY626	MALAGA	3	BOARDING
14:20	EZY7321	BELFAST INT	9	WAIT IN LOUNGE
14:35	W6206	GENEVA	24	WAIT IN LOUNGE
14:55	JEM308	BUDAPEST	12	WAIT IN LOUNGE
15:05	FR445	ISLE OF MAN	22	WAIT IN LOUNGE

The screen shows them it is time to board their plane.

They hand in their boarding cards and get on the plane.

The plane takes off for Spain.

Happy holidays!

Word bank

Look back for these words and pictures.

Airport

Assistant

Check-in

Euros

Gate

Passport

Plane

Screen

Tickets